HELP

LORD THESE EMOTIONS!

ANNETTE G. COOPER

authorHOUSE

AuthorHouse™
1663 Liberty Drive
Bloomington, IN 47403
www.authorhouse.com
Phone: 833-262-8899

Published by AuthorHouse   05/14/2021

ISBN: 978-1-6655-2602-9 (sc)
ISBN: 978-1-6655-2601-2 (e)

HELP

THE PANDEMIC 2019

1. **THE EMOTIONS I FELT**
2. **HOW DID IT AFFECT ME?**
3. **DID I EXPERIENCE FEAR OF WHAT MIGHT HAPPEN TO ME?**
4. **WHAT DID I DO DURING THE TIME I WAS LOCK DOWN IN MY HOME?**
5. **HOW DID IT AFFECT MY FAMILY MEMBERS?**
6. **WHAT HAVE I LEARNED DURING THE PANDEMIC?**
7. **CAN YOU HELP SOMEONE WHO NEEDS ENCOURAGING DURING THIS TIME?**

DID YOU PRAY?

DID YOU TRUST GOD?

ACKNOWLEDGEMENTS

First, I want to thank the Lord for all he has done for me and my family. And he still is doing great things in our life. When the enemy tried to mess with my mind, the Lord always led me to His word. He was a comforted in the time of trouble and through these trying times. "Thou wilt keep him in perfect peace, whose mind is stayed on thee: because he trusted in thee"— Isaiah 26:3. To my four children Felicia, Kerschia, Charmell, Antonio and my grandchildren and great grands whom this book is dedicated. They kept grandmother very active in their life, from going to the school to helping them in virtual school at home.

HELP

Lord these emotions!

_____
_____
_____
_____
_____
_____
_____
_____
_____
_____
_____
_____
_____
_____
_____
_____
_____
_____
_____
_____
_____
_____
_____
_____
_____
_____
_____
_____
_____
_____

What are emotions? Emotions are gifts from God. "God is Love"— John 4:8

Emotions — constantly change as circumstances changes. They may easily be misinterpreted when you are not thinking of them from a spirit-led perspective.

During this time when the world is experiencing so much turmoil, disturbance, confusion, and uncertainty. One can experience fear.

What is fear? Fear is an unpleasant emotion that can cause someone or something likely to feel afraid. The word of God lets us know that fear causes turmoil.

2 Timothy 1:7—"for God has not given us the spirit of fear, but of power and of love and of a sound mind."

We watch the news and then fear comes in because of what we see and hear. And it torments us in our mind. By God's word, he lets us know to keep our mind on him, and he will keep us in perfect peace. Isaiah 26:3—"Thou wilt keep him in perfect peace, whose mind is stayed on thee."

HELP

Lord these emotions!

_____

_____

_____

_____

_____

_____

_____

_____

_____

_____

_____

_____

_____

_____

_____

_____

_____

_____

_____

_____

_____

_____

_____

_____

_____

_____

_____

_____

_____

Doing the time being on lock down. How did the pandemic affect me emotionally? This time allowed me to appreciate the life and breathe he has given to me. It was a chance to see another day. Every minute and hour of the day is a blessing. I spend time praying for families and loved ones who are and have been affected by the pandemic. I try to keep a positive attitude and trust God each day. I try to encourage some to keep the faith, no matter how look. Trust God, and do not lean on the world system. God is your source. He will take care of me—that is his word.

For guidance we need to hear from him. Nothing will be the same anymore. This is a new era. So I have to adjust to a new way of life with the help of God—all in his will.

Proverb 3:6—"in all your ways acknowledge Him, And He shall direct your paths." (KJV)

HELP
Lord these emotions!

_____

_____

_____

_____

_____

_____

_____

_____

_____

_____

_____

_____

_____

_____

_____

_____

_____

_____

_____

_____

_____

_____

_____

_____

_____

_____

_____

_____

_____

Doing the Time on Lock Down

Not knowing what the next day would bring was not something to look forward to. People were dying all around us. The news announced how serious this pandemic was, but people were still not taking precautions. I thought about my family, my grands, and great-grands. They still did not take it serious enough to wear a mask each day. I reminded them on how important it is to protect themselves as well as others, by wearing a mask and the importance of washing their hands. In another era, it was like not the world I grew up in with no mask required. Strange for everyone to be walking around with a mask on their face. And I need the help of the Lord to get through this. A simple thing like going to the store, and you need to be at least six feet. apart from one another. Walking in the mall was excitement. Not anymore. To go with a friend or a group was out of the question. Each day reminded me of how precious life is, and how my time should be following directions from God (Proverb 3:6)—"In all thy ways acknowledge him, and He shall direct your paths."

HELP

Lord these emotions!

_____
_____
_____
_____
_____
_____
_____
_____
_____
_____
_____
_____
_____
_____
_____
_____
_____
_____
_____
_____
_____
_____
_____
_____
_____
_____
_____
_____
_____
_____

DOING THE TIME BEING ON LOCK DOWN

What was I doing this time in lock down?

I stared looking around in the home for things I should have done already. My first task was rearranging the closet from all the clutter. There was no more room for anything else away. The books and decorations in storage, and the other stuff I had accumulated was my third task I got rid of the clothes I could not wear, or would not wear from wear and tear I got rid of the nice ones and donated them to charity. Next, I made more space in my bedroom. I moved my computer desk to another place. I realized there was so much I could do in my apartment to keep in mind off the pandemic. I watched the updates just to keep in touch with what was going on around me.

HELP

Lord these emotions!

_____
_____
_____
_____
_____
_____
_____
_____
_____
_____
_____
_____
_____
_____
_____
_____
_____
_____
_____
_____
_____
_____
_____
_____
_____
_____
_____
_____
_____
_____

DOING THE TIME BEING ON LOCK DOWN

How did the pandemic effect my family members?

The pandemic affected my family members in many ways. The children were no longer in a classroom setting. Their parents were at work one day, and home the next day. No jobs to go to those who were essential workers. They were also at work one day, and home the next because someone decided to come to work sick. So that mean everyone stayed home. The parents had to assist the children now. Virtual learning was bad enough, and their attention in class was not good. Home was even worse. Being a grandmother and helping them was not an easy task, and they knew it. My question everyday was, "Are you in class?"

"Yes, grand mom," was always the answer. Until grand mom got a call. But, when he answered, they still insisted that they were in class. This went on for weeks at a time. Then school opened, and then closed. Someone got the virus. Now you, the parent and grandparent, need to be tested. School close again. Now for family members this can go on and on. You think the child can go back to school, but they are back home again, somebody got the virus.

HELP
Lord these emotions!

How did the pandemic effected my family members?

I was thinking how COVID19 took many people away, children, adults, old, young, babies—there was no age limit. Black, white, brown—color did not matter either. Lives were interrupted, people's jobs, stores, food chains, and restaurants—nothing would ever be the same. Six feet away. Mask wearing is mandatory, wearing it is a way of living. Trust is now an issue. Now you just cannot tell who's a carrier. Some people just don't care if they tested positive. They still go around people. It's a whole new way of life. Everybody is treated as a carrier until they are tested, and then being tested was so aggravating. Being swabbed so often, no one liked their nose being irritated—that's me. I work in the healthcare field, but there were some good things that happen during the pandemic. Families got closer to their kids, and spent time with their parents and their siblings, considering they were in the same household and making a stronger bond. We will continue to pray for a new beginning.

HELP
Lord these emotions!

_____
_____
_____
_____
_____
_____
_____
_____
_____
_____
_____
_____
_____
_____
_____
_____
_____
_____
_____
_____
_____
_____
_____
_____
_____
_____
_____
_____

How did the pandemic effected my family members?

Since the pandemic began in early March, in the beginning I was not super worried about it having an impact on current life as we know. When the pandemic struck last year. I was just coming off a week's vacation, in Virginia. Well, I was notified that I was going to be, laid off temporally from my job because they had limited amount of staff to work during this time. Now I was not sure how I was going to pay my bills. I had no plan set in place, in case it came to losing my job. I had to get use to not going out like to the movies, or the mall, eating or eating out in the restaurants. COVID-19 has stopped all my activities, which I enjoyed doing often. The positive side, as I look back during the time at home, was a blessing because I spend with my family. It brought us closer together because life is very precious. You only live once. I believe as a college student, I learned better online rather than in the classroom, now that is me. Because it worked out best, I am now able to schedule and balance other activities with my classes.

HELP

Lord these emotions!

_____
_____
_____
_____
_____
_____
_____
_____
_____
_____
_____
_____
_____
_____
_____
_____
_____
_____
_____
_____
_____
_____
_____
_____
_____
_____
_____
_____

Doing the time being on lock down.

I experienced the fear of the unknown.

I experienced fear that it could affect me, yes. I was scared for myself, as well as for my family members who kept doing things that they should not do. I started thinking about getting sick, shortness of breath, body aches, and pain, and all kinds of things pertaining to the pandemic. I stayed in God's word encouraging myself because you could not talk to anyone who was positive. It was never a good response, always negative.

I found myself shutting off from some people, I tried to tell them what the word of God, said concerning that he will keep us in perfect peace (John 16:33)— "These things I have spoken to you, that in Me you may have peace. In the world you will have tribulation: but be of good cheer, I have overcome the world."

But they watch and look to the news and its system, which it is their right. But for me, through it all, I put all my trust in God. When it did hit home, I prayed and he assured me we were going to come through this alright. And they did. God cannot lie, they were in his hands.

Thanks be to God.

HELP

Lord these emotions!

_____
_____
_____
_____
_____
_____
_____
_____
_____
_____
_____
_____
_____
_____
_____
_____
_____
_____
_____
_____
_____
_____
_____
_____
_____
_____
_____
_____
_____
_____

DID I PRAY AND TRUST GOD?

Doing the time on lock down.

Did I pray and trust God? The answer is yes. I did prayed without ceasing. God tells us to "Be careful, for nothing, but in everything by prayer and supplication with thanksgiving let your requests be made known unto God"—Philippians 4:6 "Pray without ceasing, don't stop praying no matter how it looks or how you feel."— 1 Thessalonians 5:17

Trust God. He is able to heal, he is able to protect you, and cover you and your family, and keep you out of harm's way. Do not look to the world for your answers. Yes, he uses man to help us. Trust God, who can save in such a time as this. Get to know God, spend time with him. Seek him. God knows all about it. "Trust in the Lord with all thine heart, and lean not unto thine own understanding. In all thy ways acknowledge him, and he shall direct thy paths."— Proverbs 3:5-6

"God will lead and guide you he cannot lie. God is not a man that he should lie; neither the son of man that he should repent: hath he said, and shall he not do it? Or hath he spoken, and shall be not make good?"—Numbers 23:19

HELP
Lord these emotions!

_____
_____
_____
_____
_____
_____
_____
_____
_____
_____
_____
_____
_____
_____
_____
_____
_____
_____
_____
_____
_____
_____
_____
_____
_____
_____
_____
_____

PRAYER

Father, God we know not what tomorrow may bring, but in your word you said, "Take therefore no thought for the morrow: for the morrow shall take thought for the things of itself."— Matthew 6:34.

"A man's hearth deviseth his way: but the Lord directeth his steps." Proverbs 16:9.

"Lord I cast all my cares upon you. You said in your word cast thy burden upon the Lord, and he shall sustain thee: he shall never suffer the righteous to be moved."— Psalms 55:22.

Guide me Lord, heal me Lord, and protect me Lord, from the evil one. Lord, I give you all the praise honor and the glory that belongs to you and you alone. Thank you, Father in the name of Jesus. Amen.

HELP

Lord these emotions!

_____
_____
_____
_____
_____
_____
_____
_____
_____
_____
_____
_____
_____
_____
_____
_____
_____
_____
_____
_____
_____
_____
_____
_____
_____
_____
_____
_____

PRAYER

Doing the time of the pandemic, Covid-19 took away many lives. All we can do is pray that we will be safe. Follow instructions, wash your hands often, stay six feet apart, and wear your masks. Let us continue to pray and give all the glory to God for keeping us safe.

HELP

Lord these emotions!

(blank lined writing space)

REFERENCE SCRIPTURE KJV

John 4:41—"And many more believed because of His own word. *Believe God at His word*".

2 Timothy 4:18—"And the Lord shall deliver me from every evil work, and will preserve me unto his heavenly kingdom: to whom be glory for ever and ever. Amen. *No matter what the enemy do God can deliver you from every evil work.*"

Isaiah 26:3—"Thou wilt keep him in perfect peace, whose mind is stayed on thee: because he trusteth in thee. *With everything going on around you keep your mind on the Lord and trust him, he will never fail you.*"

Proverb 3:6—"In all thy ways acknowledge him, and he shall direct thy paths. *Let God direct your path don't turn off the path he direct.*"

John 16:33—"These things I have spoken unto you, that in me ye might have peace. In the world ye shall have tribulation: but be of good cheer; I have overcome the world. *This means God got it all under control even though tribulation of this world.*"

Philippians 4:6—"Be careful for nothing; but in everything by prayer and supplication with thanksgiving let your requests be made known unto God. *God cares, give it to him and we pray he can answer give him thanks.*"

1 Thessalonians 5:17-18 Pray without ceasing. In everything give thanks: for this is the will of God in Christ Jesus concerning you.

Numbers 23:19—"God is not a man, that he should lie; neither the son of man, that he should repent: hath he said, and shall he not do it? or hath he spoken, and shall he not make it good?"

Matthew 6:34—"Take therefore no thought for the morrow: for the morrow shall take thought for the things of itself. Sufficient unto the day is the evil thereof."

Proverbs 16:9—"A man's heart deviseth his way: but the Lord directeth his steps."

Psalms 55:22—"Cast thy burden upon the Lord, and he shall sustain thee: he shall never suffer from the righteous to be moved."

Printed in the United States
by Baker & Taylor Publisher Services